W9-BXS-179

To Lisa —
You are the best!
I love you
♡ Allison

For my husband,
Kevin,
as it was before,
as it is now,
as it will be
into infinity...

Between Friends

written and illustrated
by

Lynne Gerard

The C.R. Gibson Company · Norwalk, CT 06856

A good friend
is like a rare shell
washed upon a
quiet beach.
        One who discovers
such a friend
finds a priceless
gift from
God.

Having a
special friend
is a true blessing,
and
evidence that
you, too, are
special.

Friends help us
know ourselves a
little better,

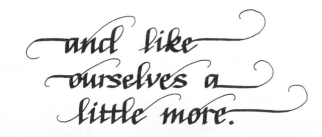

*and like
ourselves a
little more.*

Good friendships
enlighten the mind,
enrich the heart
and enhance
our lives
day to day, and
season to
season.

Friendship is as necessary as the sun, as constant as the stars and as rewarding as spring after a long winter.

One does not
go out into the
world in search
of friendship ...

friendship is something
that happens
naturally, when the
time is right, like
a rainbow in the sky.

lynne
gerard

The world is
as wide as the sky
and beyond,
and as infinite as
the twinkling
stars...

that two
kindred spirits
should come together
in friendship
is surely
evidence of
divine
intervention.

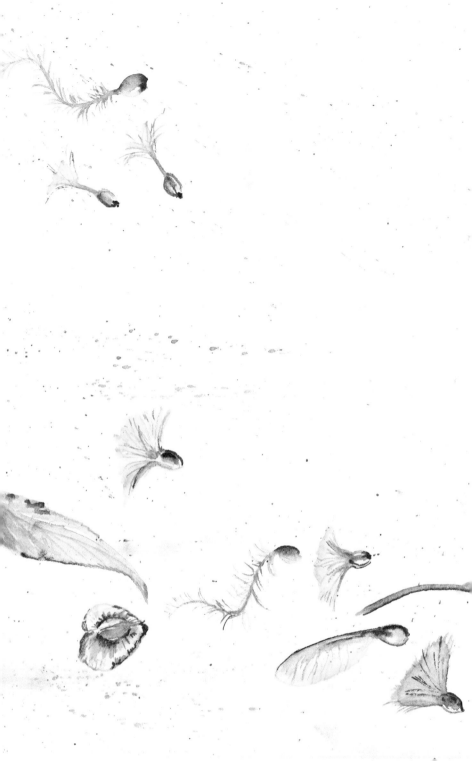

It is a fine,
divine wind that
carries a tiny
seed, just so,
and takes it
to the very
place where
friendship
needs to
grow.

Friends possess
something in
their character
that we
admire
and wish
to add to
our own
lives.

There is an
honesty between
friends that is
rare to other
relationships...

this is part
of the magic
of friendship.

With a good friend,
there is
a comfort zone
like none other,
where sharing even
silence can be
a pleasure.

The struggle to
make ends meet
in this busy,
complex world
often burdens our
hearts...
friendship
helps soften
the hard edge
of
life.

Good friendships
contain the strength
of affection
that makes
forgiveness instantaneous,
and disappointment
forgotten.

Good friendships
are not
measured by the
frequency of
phone calls,
or letters
or visits...

Lynne
Gerard

the
best
friendships
are recognized
by the quality
of
time and
feelings
shared.

Friendships
grow deeper as
trust and
cooperation
evolve from
shared
experiences ...

lynne
gerard

There is a place, between friends, for seriousness as well as humor, and countless ways to show appreciation.

Time passes by
and steals the
days and years.
Changes are
many, and often...
they always will
be... but a good
friendship lasts
a lifetime.

.